The Big Catch

David Mackenzie

Nelson

Exercises and a glossary can be found at the back of the book.

Thomas Nelson and Sons Ltd
Nelson House Mayfield Road
Walton-on-Thames Surrey
KT12 5PL UK

51 York Place
Edinburgh
EH1 3JD UK

Thomas Nelson (Hong Kong) Ltd
Toppan Building 10/F
22A Westlands Road
Quarry Bay Hong Kong

© David Mackenzie 1991
Exercises and Activities © Jeremy Hunter 1991

First published by Thomas Nelson and Sons Ltd 1991

ISBN 0-17-555980-5
NPN 9 8 7 6 5 4 3 2 1

Illustrations by Derek Worrall

All rights reserved. This publication is protected in the United Kingdom
by the Copyright Act 1956 and in other countries by comparable
legislation. No part of it may be reproduced or recorded by any means
without the permission of the publisher. This prohibition extends (with
certain very limited exceptions) to photocopying and similar processes,
and written permission to make a copy or copies must therefore be
obtained from the publisher in advance. It is advisable to consult the
publisher if there is any doubt regarding the legality of any proposed
copying.

Printed in Hong Kong

Chapter One

The Old Man and the Sea

I thought it was going to be difficult. But it was easy.

I was looking for a man, a fishing-boat captain called Simeon, and I found him. No, that's not exactly right. *I* didn't find *him*. *He* found *me*.

But I knew where to look for him. I went to the port of Filder and I visited the bars. I visited three without finding him. Then I went into a bar called The Old Man and The Sea.

The inside of the bar was dark and full of cigarette smoke. There were only a few men there, and no women. It was not the kind of bar that women go to. Only men go there and most of them are sailors. I had never even been on a boat in my life. I didn't feel comfortable in the bar. I ordered a drink and decided to finish it quickly and leave.

Three hours later I was still in The Old Man and The Sea. This is what happened:

As I stood with my glass in my hand, a man came

The Big Catch

up to me. 'Will you listen to me?' he asked.

I looked at him. He was about sixty or sixty-five, with grey hair and a grey beard. He was wearing a thick white pullover and a blue jacket. He was clearly a sailor and he was clearly not sober.

'Will you listen to me?' he asked again.

'I don't think so,' I said.

He called to the barman. 'Give this man a drink.'

'I've got a drink,' I said.

'Then have another one.'

'Thank you,' I said. 'But I only want one.'

But the barman gave me another drink. He put the glass in front of me, next to the one I already had.

'Drink some of that,' the old sailor said.

'Why?' I asked.

'Because then I can tell you my name,' he said. 'And then I can tell you my story.'

'But I have to drink first?'

'That's right.'

I took the second glass. I held it in my hand but I didn't drink. 'Your story,' I said, 'is it a good story?'

He laughed. 'A good story! A good story!' He looked at the barman. 'Tell him, John.'

The barman turned to me. 'It's a good story,' he said.

I drank from the glass the old sailor gave me.

The Big Catch

'My name's Simeon,' the old man said. 'People call me Sim. I was a sailor, a captain.'

'You're not a captain now?' I asked.

'No, I'm not,' he said. 'I had my own boat. For twelve years I had my own boat.' He took a very old photograph from his wallet and gave it to me. It was a photograph of a fishing-boat, a big fishing-boat.

'She was called the *Eldessa*,' Sim said. 'I had her for twelve years.'

'That's a long time,' I said. 'So you haven't got her now?'

'No,' he said and he took another drink from his glass.

'Did she sink?' I asked.

He laughed. 'No,' he said. 'She didn't sink.'

'Then what happened?'

'They took her away from me,' he said. He stopped laughing.

'Why did they do that?' I asked.

'I did something very bad,' he said. 'I did the worst thing that a fishing captain can do.'

'What's that?'

Sim finished his drink. 'I didn't bring home any fish,' he said.

'Oh, for years I caught lots of fish,' Sim went on. 'Yes, lots of fish. I knew the best places to go and I

The Big Catch

The Big Catch

caught lots of fish. I was a good fisherman. As I said, I bought my own boat, the *Eldessa*. Then, thirty-three years ago, everything changed.'

'Thirty-three years ago,' I said. 'That's a long time.'

'It is,' he said.

'How did things change?'

'I took the boat out and we stayed on the sea for a week. Usually we go out for four days but we stayed for a week and we caught nothing.'

'Nothing?'

'Nothing at all. I took the *Eldessa* to the best places – the places where we *always* caught fish – but we caught nothing. Not even a sardine. So we came home. We came home without any fish.'

'What happened then?' I asked.

'We went out again two days later. We came back with no fish. Then we went out a third time. Again, no fish.'

'What about the other fishing-boats?' I asked. 'Did they catch fish?'

'Lots. Thousands of fish. I was the only one who couldn't catch fish. People said it was just bad luck. "Keep fishing," they said. "Keep trying." Then, after my third trip with no fish they began to think it was *very* bad luck. *Very, very* bad luck. They began to think there was something wrong with me. Some of my friends didn't speak to me.'

'Why not?' I asked.

'They didn't want to get bad luck from me.'

'Nice friends,' I said.

'So, I decided to make one more trip.'

'The fourth?'

'That's right. The fourth trip. I had to catch fish this time. I had to. If not ... well, goodbye to the *Eldessa,* goodbye to the sea, goodbye to Sim ...'

'And did you catch any fish on the fourth trip?' I asked.

Sim laughed. He laughed for half a minute. I turned to the barman and asked for two more drinks.

Sim said, 'Fish? Fish?' He was smiling. 'I caught more fish than ever before. I caught tens of thousands of fish. The *Eldessa* was full of fish. There were fish everywhere.'

'So,' I said. 'That was good, wasn't it?'

'No,' Sim said. 'It wasn't good. It was bad, very bad. In fact it was terrible.' He wasn't smiling now.

'I don't understand,' I said.

'Well,' Sim said. 'Do you want to hear the whole story?'

I looked at my watch. But I had nowhere else to go now. The barman gave us new drinks. I put one of them in front of Sim. 'Yes,' I said. 'Tell me the whole story.'

The Big Catch

Chapter Two

Sim's Story - The Clock and the Dolphin

There were four of us on the *Eldessa* - an old man called George Millfield, known as 'Middy', a man of about thirty called Bill Shell, a young boy called Alan and me. Alan was only sixteen. Middy, the boat's engineer, Bill and Alan weren't very happy because they had no money. Three trips without fish meant no money. This time we had to catch fish. We had to.

We started at just after midnight on a Monday morning. Fishermen never start their trips on a Sunday. Starting on a Sunday is bad luck. That was the first problem. When we were leaving the port Middy said, 'The boat's clock is wrong.'

I checked the time. The boat's clock said 12.10 but my watch said 12.05. I knew my watch was right. Alan and Bill joined us in the wheelhouse where the boat's clock was.

'We started before midnight,' Middy said and I knew he was unhappy. 'We started on a Sunday.'

'Bad luck,' Middy said. 'Very bad luck.'

The Big Catch

'Don't be silly,' Bill said.

I said nothing.

When morning came we were already thirty miles out at sea. In the east the sky was red and I knew this meant trouble. The sea wasn't blue, it was dark grey, with thin lines of white at the tops of the waves. The wind grew stronger. The waves became higher and their tops became whiter. It began to rain. The *Eldessa* moved more slowly and went up and down on the waves. Alan became afraid. It was his first storm.

I sent Alan below with Middy. Bill and I stayed in the wheelhouse. I changed the engine speed to slow and we went forward into the waves. The sky was now dark grey. The drops of rain hit the windows of the wheelhouse like bullets. Bill tried to speak to me but it was impossible to hear him.

In front of the *Eldessa* I could see waves as big as mountains.

Four hours later, the storm ended. The sea grew calmer and the sky changed from grey to blue. All four of us were very tired. Bill and I went below and slept for a few hours. Then Alan and Middy slept. We had a meal together late in the day.

'I told you,' Middy said. 'We started on Sunday and that was bad luck.'

'But we're OK,' Alan said. 'The storm is over and we're OK.'

The Big Catch

'Alan's right,' I said, but Bill and Middy didn't say anything.

'Tomorrow,' I said, 'we start fishing and we're going to catch lots of fish. Lots of fish.' I smiled. Alan smiled too but the other two didn't.

On Tuesday the sea was calm. We started fishing at five o'clock in the morning and we fished all day. We put the net out eleven times. We fished and fished and fished until we were asleep on our feet. We stopped fishing at seven o'clock in the evening.

So, we fished for fourteen hours, and we caught nothing.

When we had dinner together we were all unhappy. Except Alan. He was tired but he said, 'Tomorrow we'll catch fish. I know we will.'

'I don't understand,' Middy said. 'Why can't we catch anything?'

'I don't understand either,' Bill said.

'Alan's right,' I said. 'We'll catch fish soon. Tomorrow.' I said this, but I didn't believe it.

On Wednesday the sea was flat and silver like glass. There were no waves. The sky was blue and the sun was hot. The *Eldessa* sat on the water and didn't move. I said to myself, 'The world has stopped.'

The sky, the sea, the air, everything was

beautiful. I think we all felt happy, but we all knew there were no fish.

But we fished anyway. We put the net out once, twice, three times and we caught nothing. The fourth time, however, everything was different. As we pulled in the net it was heavy, very heavy.

'Fish!' Alan shouted. 'Fish!'

'Yes, yes, yes!!' Bill said. Even Middy was able to smile.

We pulled in the net as fast as we could. But as we pulled it in we knew something was wrong. We usually caught herring. Herring are small silver fish. We caught thousands of them in one net. But this time we knew we didn't have herring in the net. No, we didn't have lots of fish, we had only one fish, one very big fish.

But it wasn't a fish. It was a dolphin.

We pulled it out of the water and dropped it onto the deck of the *Eldessa*. The dolphin was very big. It was long and grey and it looked very beautiful. It was still alive.

'Throw it back,' Middy said.

'Yes, throw it back,' said Alan.

'Can we sell it?' Bill asked.

I looked down at the dolphin. It was trying to swim but it couldn't. I felt sorry for it. But I said, 'Yes, we can sell it.'

'Then kill it,' Bill said.

'No, don't kill it,' said Alan.

'Alan,' said Bill, 'we haven't got anything else. We haven't got any money. We can't throw it back.'

I looked at Middy. 'Killing a dolphin is bad luck,' he said.

I went to the wheelhouse to get my knife. Alan followed me. 'Please don't kill it,' he said. 'Please don't.'

'I'm sorry Alan,' I said.

I found my knife and I went back to the dolphin. Lying on the deck it looked very sad and very beautiful. I stood on one side of it. Bill and Middy stood on the other side. Alan was still in the wheelhouse.

'Go on,' Bill said.

Middy said nothing.

I didn't want to kill the dolphin. I really didn't want to kill it. But I did.

The Big Catch

Chapter Three

Sim's Story - The Silver Herring

For the rest of Wednesday we fished but we caught nothing. The dead dolphin looked at us from the deck. By the end of the day I felt it was watching me and I hated it. In the evening I said, 'Put it below.' Bill and Middy pulled it over to the hatch and it fell into the hold.

We put the net out twice more but caught nothing.

'OK,' I said at nine o'clock. 'Let's move. We'll go north and we'll try there. We'll sail during the night and we'll begin fishing in the morning.'

Middy went below to start the engine. I went to the wheelhouse and waited. Five minutes later, Middy came to the wheelhouse.

'Something's wrong,' he said. 'The engine won't start.'

'What do you mean?' I asked.

'It won't start,' he said. 'I don't know what's wrong, but it won't start. It's broken.' He was angry.

'You're the engineer,' I said. 'Repair it.' I was

The Big Catch

angry too.

Middy went below.

Two hours later the engine was still broken.

'I don't know what's wrong,' Middy said. He was more tired than angry now. 'I can't repair it.'

'We need help,' Bill said.

'Yes,' I said. 'We can't stay here forever.'

'Give me another hour,' Middy said.

He went below again but he couldn't repair the engine. At midnight I knew we had to get help. I switched on the boat's radio.

'This is the *Eldessa*,' I said into the radio. 'This is the *Eldessa*. Our engine is broken. We need help. We need help.'

All four of us were in the wheelhouse. We listened hard to the radio but we couldn't hear anything.

'There must be someone somewhere out there,' Bill said. 'There are lost of fishing-boats out there.'

'Yes, there are,' I said. 'There are lots of boats but they can't hear us.'

'Why not?' asked Alan.

I looked at the radio. 'Because the radio is broken too,' I said.

On Thursday the sea was calm again and the sky was blue. It was very hot and we all felt very

The Big Catch

uncomfortable.

The *Eldessa* couldn't move and we couldn't radio for help. Middy stayed below all day and tried to repair the engine but he failed. Alan tried to repair the radio but he couldn't.

At seven o'clock in the evening all four of us met to decide what to do.

'I don't understand,' Alan said. 'The engine *and* the radio. Why are they both broken?'

'The dolphin,' Middy said. 'We killed the dolphin. That's bad luck.'

Bill laughed. 'And we left on Sunday. That's bad luck too, isn't it, Middy?'

'It is,' said Middy.

'Oh, you're crazy,' Bill said. 'You're a crazy old man, Middy.'

'So what do we do?' Alan asked.

'Throw the dolphin back into the sea,' Middy said.

'No,' Bill said. He wasn't laughing any more.

'Throw it into the sea,' Middy said again.

'And then the engine will be OK?' I asked. 'And the radio?' I smiled, though I tried not to.

'Yes,' Middy said.

'Help him, Alan,' I said.

Bill laughed again.

'You help him too, Bill,' I said, and he stopped laughing. All three went below.

The Big Catch

It was very difficult to pull the dolphin up to the deck from the hold. It was very heavy. It took Bill, Alan and Middy more than half an hour but they were successful. I looked at the dolphin. Once it was a beautiful living thing. Now it was ugly, dead meat. Also it smelt bad.

'Throw it in the sea,' I said.

They took it to the side. It fell into the sea with a big splash. We watched it as it sank very slowly. We watched it for a full minute until we couldn't see it any more.

Middy went below into the engine room. He repaired the engine in half an hour.

It was time to go back to Filder but we didn't turn back. I wanted fish. On Thursday night and into Friday morning we sailed north. The weather was fine and the engine was OK. The radio was still broken but we all felt happier. 'We must catch fish,' I said to myself. 'We *will* catch fish.'

We started fishing at five o'clock on Friday morning. We fished till noon. Nothing.

'Don't worry,' I said. 'There are fish in there for us.' I was sure of that. I knew there were fish for us that day.

We turned west and sailed for two hours. The wind grew stronger but not too strong. The sea wasn't calm any more. But everything looked good.

The Big Catch

The *Eldessa* moved well over the waves. At two o'clock we started fishing again.

The first time we put the net out I knew this was our lucky day. We pulled in the net and it was full of fish, full of beautiful silver herring. We all laughed as we pulled in the net and dropped the herring into the hold.

'More!' Bill shouted and we hurried to put the net out again. Again the net was heavy, very heavy. It was heavier than the first time. Even Middy was laughing. We couldn't believe it. The net was full of herring.

That day we put the net out six more times and we caught herring every time. At nine o'clock that evening we were all very tired. But we were very happy. The hold was full of herring, more herring than ever before.

As I fell asleep that night I thought, 'What can go wrong now?'

Chapter Four

Sim's Story - The Propeller, the Net and the Knife

I wanted more. That's what went wrong. I wanted too much.

In the morning, early, I said, 'Let's put the net out one more time.'

'But the hold is full,' Alan said. 'We can't put any more fish there.'

'Alan's right,' Middy said. 'It's time to go back to Filder.'

Bill said, 'There's enough space for some more fish – one more net.'

'OK,' I said, 'let's do it.'

We put the net out. As we pulled it in I knew we had a problem. The net was heavier than ever before. It was very difficult to pull it in because there were thousands of herring in it. It was almost impossible to lift it from the sea. I was sure something was going to break.

The rope holding the net broke. The net fell, hit the deck of the Eldessa and then fell back into the sea. All the fish escaped.

The Big Catch

All four of us stood on the deck and looked down at the broken net.

'Pull it in,' I said. I looked at the other three. They were all unhappy. Middy was angry too, but he said nothing.

'Let's go home,' I said.

Middy went below to start the engine. Bill and Alan began to pull in the net. I went to the wheelhouse.

Then Bill shouted, 'We can't pull in the net.'

I stepped out of the wheelhouse. 'Why not?'

Alan was looking into the water. 'I think it's round the propeller,' he said.

I ran to the engine-room hatch and shouted to Middy, 'Middy, don't …!' But it was too late. Middy started the engine. The net went round and round the propeller until the propeller stopped.

Middy looked up from the hatch. 'What's wrong?' he asked.

'The net's round the propeller,' I said. 'Switch off the engine.' He switched it off.

Two minutes later we were looking down at the propeller. It was impossible to see it. All we saw was the net.

'Well,' Bill said, 'we can't move until we free the propeller.'

'That's right,' I said.

The Big Catch

'How can we do that?' Alan asked.

Middy said, 'Someone must go down there and cut the net. Can you swim?' he asked Alan.

'No, I can't,' Alan said. 'Can you?'

'No.' Middy looked at Bill who said, 'No' also.

All three looked at me.

'I can't swim either,' I said.

For two days the *Eldessa* didn't move. We tried everything to free the propeller but we failed. The problem was that the propeller was deep in the water. I put a knife on the end of a long stick and I cut some of the net but not all of it. It was very difficult indeed.

The sea was calm and the sky blue. It was very hot. By the end of the second day, Monday, we had another problem: there was a very bad smell coming from the hold.

'All the fish,' said Bill, 'all those beautiful fish – now they're all bad.'

Bill and Middy looked very fed up. I thought Alan was going to cry. I felt more miserable than ever before.

'Well,' I said, 'there's only one thing we can do.'

They knew what I meant.

That evening we threw all the fish back into the sea.

The Big Catch

The next morning the *Eldessa* sat in the middle of thousands of dead fish. There were thousands of sea-birds too. They flew down to take the fish from the water. I watched them for a long time. Bad luck for us meant good luck for them.

Then Alan shouted, 'Look!'

He was looking at the propeller. We saw the net clearly now. As there were no fish in the hold the *Eldessa* was not so deep in the water.

'Right,' I said. 'Bring me a rope.' Now I had a plan.

With one end of the rope round me I jumped into the sea. Bill and Middy held the other end. For a few seconds I was underwater. Then Bill and Middy pulled the rope and I came up to the top. For two minutes I coughed and coughed.

'I don't like this!' I shouted up to them.

'Be careful!' Alan shouted.

I smiled. 'I'll be OK,' I said.

With my knife I began cutting the net. Most of the net was out of the water but some of it was not. I worked for an hour; cutting, cutting, cutting ... Then they pulled me up onto the deck for a rest. I was very tired.

'I'll go down,' Alan said. 'You have a rest. I'll go down.'

'No,' I said, and I stood up. 'It's my problem. I'll

The Big Catch

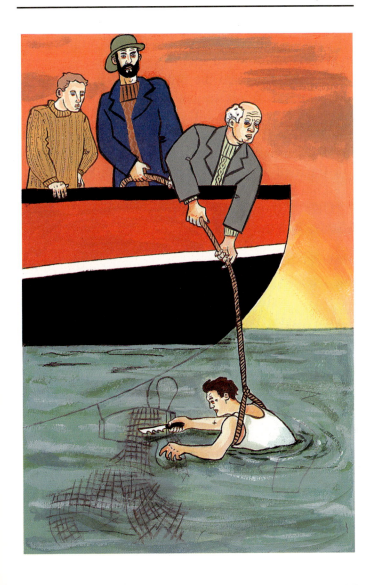

go down again.' I rested for fifteen minutes and then went into the sea again.

As I got closer to the propeller, it became more and more difficult to cut the net. I worked for another hour. Now I sometimes had to go underwater. I cut and cut and cut. At eight o'clock in the evening I asked for another knife.

I finished at nine o'clock. It was dark and I was tired but the propeller was free.

'OK!' I shouted. It was too dark to see Bill and Middy, but they still held the rope. 'Everything's OK. Pull me up!'

They began to pull me up, but then something happened to the rope. I fell back into the sea.

'No!' I shouted but my head went under the water. I came back to the top, coughing. 'No! No! No! Help!' But I was a few metres from the *Eldessa* and I couldn't see anything. 'Help!' I shouted again. 'Help! Help!'

Then I heard Middy starting the engine. The *Eldessa* began to move away from me.

Chapter Five

Sim's Story - The Raft

I knew I was going to die.

I shouted and shouted but no one answered. I knew that in one minute, perhaps two, I was going to die. The pieces of net round me helped to keep my head out of the water. But I tasted sea water in my mouth.

It was difficult to see anything because it was late and the sky was dark. But I saw the boat, my boat, moving away. The *Eldessa* was something big and black on the water in front of me. Then it was not so big. Then it became smaller and smaller.

Something splashed in the water beside me. I tried to move towards it. It was on top of the water. I held onto it. A piece of wood. It helped me to keep my head out of the water.

I shouted. I felt sea water in my mouth. I coughed. I held onto the piece of wood . I shouted again. It was impossible to see the *Eldessa* now. I shouted one more time. I tried to understand what was happening.

I looked but I saw nothing.

The Big Catch

The Big Catch

I listened but I heard nothing.
I stopped shouting.

The piece of wood helped me. I wasn't sure if that was better or worse. Perhaps I wasn't going to die in two minutes. Perhaps I was going to die in two hours. Was that better?

I tried to lie on top of the piece of wood but it was too small. I wanted to get out of the water but it was impossible. I was tired and I wanted something to eat. I was thirsty too, but I knew it was impossible to drink sea water. I held onto the piece of wood and I waited.

During the night I fell asleep many times. But each time my head went under the water I woke up immediately.

In the morning I felt very weak. I looked round and I saw pieces of net and some more pieces of wood. When I saw the wood I began to feel a little better. Very slowly I moved in the water. I got one piece of wood, then another and then another. In an hour I had seven or eight pieces of wood. I used pieces of the net to hold the wood together. So now I had a raft. I pulled myself on top of it. For the first time for ten hours I was out of the water. I lay on top of the raft and I fell asleep.

I can't remember much after that. I lay on the raft

The Big Catch

for one day - perhaps two. Then another fishing boat, the *Rose*, found me. The captain of the *Rose* was a man called Peter Minton. I knew him well but I can't remember anything about my trip on the *Rose*. He took me back to the nearest port, the town of Branden. I nearly died on the trip. When we got to Branden he took me to hospital. I was very ill and I stayed in hospital for two weeks.

After two weeks I left the hospital but it took me two or three weeks more to get well again. I went back to Filder. In those five weeks no one saw the *Eldessa*. She didn't come back to Filder or to Branden. She didn't come back to any of the ports on this part of the coast.

The *Eldessa* disappeared.

I decided that Middy and Bill – and perhaps Alan too – were all bad men. They took away my boat, my beautiful *Eldessa*, and they left me in the sea to die. Now I had no fish, no boat, no job. I didn't have much money either. I didn't know what to do. I wanted to find the *Eldessa* but I didn't know how to. The sea is big; the *Eldessa* was small. Where was the best place to start looking?

I started to drink. So I came to the pub every day and I drank. I drank wine because it was cheap. I drank bottles and bottles of wine. At the weekend I drank more. I wasn't sober from Friday night to

The Big Catch

Monday morning.

After two or three weeks of this I had no money. I asked my friends for money and they lent me some. I bought more wine. I tried to borrow more money but it was difficult. My friends didn't want to give me money just for wine. They were right, of course, but I didn't understand then. I asked for more money and they said no. I asked all of them, every day, many times a day. They said no.

So, two or three months after the fourth trip of the *Eldessa* I had no fish, no boat, no job, no money and no friends. I was the most miserable man in the world.

But someone found the *Eldessa*. A fishing boat called the *Marsa* went far to the north and found her. There was no one on the *Eldessa* - no Middy, no Bill, no Alan. The boat was empty and it was in the middle of the sea. Where were Middy, Bill and Alan?

Nobody knew. The captain of the *Marsa* didn't see them. He took the *Eldessa* back to Branden. I went down to see them arrive. The *Marsa* pulled the *Eldessa* slowly back into port.

But I was sad. She wasn't my boat any more. I had no money to pay the bank. Now the bank was the owner of the *Eldessa*. One week later the *Eldessa* had a new captain. He took her out to sea and he stayed away for five days. I went down to see him arrive back. I saw that the *Eldessa* was moving very slowly. I knew what that meant. She was full of fish. I watched them bringing the fish from the hold. There were thousands of them, thousands and thousands of silver herring.

I went to the pub to drink more wine ...

Chapter Six

A Dying Man

'That's the end of my story,' Sim said.

'Is it?' I asked. It was late. The barman was ready to close the bar.

'Yes, it is,' Sim said. In front of him there was another glass of wine – his sixth or seventh.

'But that was thirty-three years ago,' I said. 'What happened from then until now?'

Sim held his glass of wine in front of his face. 'This,' he said. 'This is what happened. This is what happens all the time.'

'Tell me about Alan,' I said.

'Alan?' Sim thought for a few seconds. 'Alan was a good man. I liked Alan. I think about him often. Perhaps Bill and Middy wanted to kill me but not Alan. No, not Alan. It's not possible.'

'When did you last see him?' I asked.

'Thirty-three years ago, on the *Eldessa*. I haven't seen him since then. Nor Bill … nor Middy.'

We stood quietly for a few moments.

'I know Alan,' I said. Nearly a minute passed before Sim understood.

'You! ... you know Alan?' he asked.
'He's my father,' I said.
'Alan? Alan from the *Eldessa?*'
'That's right.'
'But ... but where is he?'
'Not far from here.'
'Really?'
'Yes. And he wants to see you.'

Sim took his glass of wine. He put it to his mouth but he didn't drink. He put the glass down again.

'I want to see him too,' Sim said.
'Good,' I said. I finished my drink. Then I said, 'But there's one problem.'
'Oh? Is there?'
'Yes,' I said, 'Alan is dying.'

'I can't come now,' Sim said.
'Why not?' I asked.
'Too much of this,' he said. He held his glass up. 'I'm not sober.' He put down his glass again without finishing his wine. 'Come on. Come with me.'

It was ten thirty when we left The Old Man and The Sea. Sim took me down some dark little streets. We walked for ten or fifteen minutes. We came to a white building with a red door. We went in. We sat down in a small, dark room. An old woman came in.

'Is that you, Sim?' she asked.

'Yes,' said Sim.

'It's late,' the old woman said. 'What do you want?'

'Coffee,' Sim replied, 'black coffee.'

The old woman laughed. 'Coffee? Are you sure? Don't you want some wine?'

'No,' Sim said.

'And your friend?'

'I'll have coffee too,' I said.

The old woman left.

'But Alan is still young,' Sim said as we drank our coffee. 'He's younger than me.'

'Forty-nine,' I said. 'But he's very ill. He's going to die soon.'

'How soon?'

'Next month. Next week. Perhaps tomorrow,' I said.

'I'm sorry,' Sim said.

'He's a very unhappy man,' I said.

'I can understand,' Sim said.

'No, I don't mean he's just unhappy about dying. No. I mean he's unhappy about dying *without seeing you.* He wants to tell you what happened.'

'What do *you* know?' Sim asked.

'Nothing,' I said. 'Nothing until today.'

'Nothing at all?'

The Big Catch

'Nothing.'

Sim finished his coffee and filled up his cup again. He drank the second cup quickly. 'OK,' he said. 'Let's go.'

We went back to the little streets. But this time Sim followed me. I took him to the house where my father and I were staying.

'How long have you been here?' Sim asked.

'Only a month,' I said. 'We were in America before that.'

'America?'

'Yes,' I said. 'Alan went to America thirty years ago. I was born there.'

We arrived at the door of my father's room.

'I'm afraid,' Sim said.

'Don't be,' I said. 'My father's afraid too. But he must see you.'

We went in.

My father was not old, but he looked old. He was lying in bed. He looked small and sick and very old. His hair was white.

'Alan?' Sim said. 'Is that you, Alan?'

'I ...'

'Yes? ...'

'I threw the wood,' the old man said. My father. Alan. 'I threw the piece of wood. You know that, don't you?'

The Big Catch

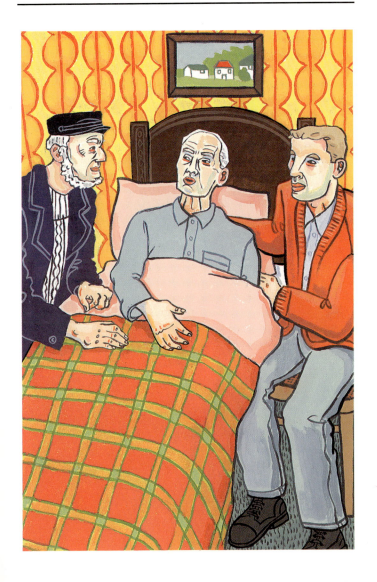

'Yes,' said Sim.
'I wanted to save you; I didn't want to kill you.'
'I know.'
'Bill and Middy, they wanted to kill you.'
'What happened to them?' Sim asked.

My father looked at Sim with tired eyes. 'Sit down,' he said, 'and I'll tell you the whole story.'

Chapter Seven

Alan's Story : The New Captain

I threw the piece of wood to you and then someone pulled my arm. It was Bill. 'Why did you do that?' he asked. He was very angry.

'But he'll die,' I said. 'Do you want Sim to die?'

'Yes,' Bill said, 'I do.'

At that moment Middy started the engine. 'No!' I shouted. I ran to the side of the *Eldessa*. I looked down into the sea. I saw the white water over the propeller but that was all. I couldn't see you. It was too dark.

Then Middy was beside me. 'Do you want Sim to die too?' I asked him. Middy said nothing. I saw that he was unhappy. He didn't like what was happening.

'Stop the boat,' I said. 'Stop her. We must go back.' Middy wasn't sure what to do. 'Go on,' I said again. 'Stop the boat.'

'No!' said Bill. He was standing in front of Middy. He had a knife in his hand. It was a knife like yours, Sim. I remembered the dolphin. I remembered how easily you killed the dolphin with that knife. I began to feel afraid.

Middy and I understood that Bill was the new captain of the *Eldessa*. He told Middy to go to the wheelhouse. Middy went. Then he took me to the hold. I opened the hatch and went down inside. Bill closed the hatch over me and locked it. The hold was completely dark and it smelled of fish. After a few moments I understood that I couldn't get out of the hold. I was in prison.

The next morning Bill opened the hatch. The light hurt my eyes. He helped me up onto the deck.

'Where are we?' I said.

'Don't ask,' Bill replied. 'Go to the galley and cook breakfast.'

I stood in the galley for a few minutes. I tried to decide what to do. Bill looked dangerous. I didn't want to make him angry. I remembered the knife. It was Bill, I decided. Bill was the bad man. Middy was OK. I decided to try and speak to Middy alone without Bill. I knew this was going to be difficult.

I cooked a good breakfast: bacon, eggs, tomatoes, toast, coffee. I took everything up on deck. It was a beautiful morning. The sky was blue and the sea was calm. The air smelled good. For a moment I felt happy. I tried to sound happy too. Bill and Middy were both in the wheelhouse. 'Breakfast!' I said as I went in.

'Good,' Bill said. He took his plate.

The Big Catch

I looked at Middy. Middy had a black eye. 'What happened to you?' I said.

But it was Bill who replied. 'You fell, didn't you, Middy?'

Middy looked at Bill, then at me. 'That's right,' he said, 'I fell.'

I gave Middy his plate. All three of us finished our breakfast in the wheelhouse. No one spoke.

It was difficult to speak to Middy. Bill was always there and he knew we wanted to talk together. He gave us jobs to do that kept us at different ends of the boat. When I was in the wheelhouse, Middy was in the galley. Once, when we passed each other, Middy said one word. 'Radio.'

The radio was in the wheelhouse but it was still broken. I decided to try to repair it.

For the next two days we sailed north again. Bill didn't say exactly where we were going. I cooked the food in the galley and Middy stayed in the engine-room most of the time. Bill was in the wheelhouse.

In the afternoon of the second day, Middy asked Bill to come to the engine-room. While they were together, I went to the wheelhouse. I looked at the radio. Perhaps I could repair it. I took the top off

The Big Catch

and looked inside. I didn't know how to begin. I looked hard for two or three minutes. Then I heard Bill coming back to the wheelhouse. I put the top back on the radio quickly.

Later I quietly said to Middy, 'I need more time with the radio.'

'OK,' Middy said.

The next morning, I tried again. Middy and Bill were in the engine-room. I took the top off the radio and thought hard. I touched one or two things inside. I really didn't know what to do. I put the top back and switched the radio on. The light came on! I don't know how I repaired it, but the radio was OK! Now I could radio for help.

I began to speak but at that moment Bill came into the wheelhouse behind me. I was very afraid but Bill spoke calmly.

'Forget the radio,' he said. Then he pulled it onto the floor of the wheelhouse. He broke the radio with his heavy boots. 'Come with me,' he said.

He locked me in the hold and I stayed there for two days. I had nothing to eat and nothing to drink. I felt tired and miserable and very, very thirsty. On the third morning Bill let me out of the hold. The light was so strong I couldn't see anything. He gave me some water. Then he told me to go to the galley to cook breakfast.

I felt very weak. First I ate some bread. It was old

bread, but it tasted delicious. Then I cooked breakfast.

I took three plates of food to the wheelhouse. Bill was there. I gave him his plate. I went out on deck again. 'Middy!' I shouted. 'Breakfast!' I turned to the open door of the wheelhouse. 'Where's Middy?' I asked.

'He's not here,' Bill said.

'Not here?' I didn't understand.

'He left during the night,' Bill said and he smiled. He didn't look angry any more. He looked crazy.

Chapter Eight

Alan's Story : Killing a Dolphin

So now there was only me and Bill on the *Eldessa*. We sailed for three days. I didn't know where we were going. We didn't talk to each other. Bill stayed in the wheelhouse most of the time. I stayed in the galley and cooked the meals. Sometimes I went down to look at the engine. At night Bill locked me in the hold.

Life on the *Eldessa* was very difficult. I couldn't attack Bill - he was too strong. Anyway, he always carried his knife. I was weak and I felt miserable. We had very little food left. I didn't know what to do.

I'm sure Bill didn't know what to do either. He didn't really know where to go. We sailed north. When we saw another boat he turned the *Eldessa* away.

Then, in the afternoon of the third day, I saw land. It was a small island two or three miles from the *Eldessa*. There were a few houses. I saw some boats, too. I began to feel better.

I turned to Bill. 'Are we going there?' I asked.

The Big Catch

'Not *we*,' Bill said. '*I'm* going there, but you're not.' He had the knife in his hand and I saw that crazy look in his eyes.

'No!' I said, 'don't do it!' I ran to the side of the boat. Bill followed. He caught me and held the knife at my throat. 'No!' I shouted. 'No!' I pulled the knife away from my throat and ran to the other side of the boat. Bill followed again. But before he got close to me I jumped over the side into the sea.

As I hit the water I heard Bill laughing. 'You can't swim!' he laughed. 'You can't swim!'

But he was wrong. You see, I lied to you, Sim, when you wanted help with the propeller. I said I couldn't swim. It wasn't true. I *can* swim. I lied because I was afraid. I didn't want to go into the sea.

This time I had no choice. There was Bill with the knife, or the sea. So I jumped into the sea. But I swam down under the boat and came up on the other side. Bill didn't see me. I held onto a rope on the side of the boat and I waited.

I waited for half an hour. We didn't go to the island. Perhaps Bill wasn't ready. He needed a good story to tell the people on the island. Perhaps he decided he didn't want to meet anyone.

I heard him moving on deck. I heard him going into the wheelhouse and I heard him in the galley.

The Big Catch

Then I heard him going down to the engine-room. I pulled myself up on the rope, very slowly. I got onto the deck. I was cold and wet and very tired but I knew what I had to do. I had to kill Bill.

I found a short, heavy piece of wood and I waited outside the engine-room door. I waited for ten minutes and they were the longest ten minutes of my life. I was cold and wet and I didn't feel very strong, but I knew I had to do it. I had to kill him.

I heard him coming up from the engine-room. When he arrived at the door he stopped. He was on one side of the door and I was on the other. A few long seconds passed. He went back down into the engine-room. I began to feel afraid. Did he know I was there? Perhaps the knife was in the engine-room and he was going back down to get it. Another two minutes passed. I heard him coming up the steps again. The door opened.

He turned and for a moment he looked at me in complete surprise. Then I hit him in the face as hard as I could with the piece of wood.

I can still remember the terrible sound of the wood hitting Bill's face. I will never forget it. Bill fell back down the steps into the engine-room. From the top of the steps I saw him lying on the engine-room floor. There was a lot of blood on the floor by his head. He wasn't moving, but I had to

The Big Catch

wait for a full minute before I went down; I was too afraid.

But I went down because I had to stop the engine. Also I couldn't leave him lying there. I had to bring him up to the deck. It was very difficult. Bill was a big man and very heavy. I knew I couldn't carry him. Very slowly I pulled him up the steps, one by one. It took me fifteen minutes to do this.

When I got him onto the deck, I rested for five minutes. I couldn't look at him. His face was terrible. Then I pulled him to the side of the boat. I let him fall into the sea.

I watched him as he sank slowly in the water. I remembered watching the dolphin after you had killed it. Killing a dolphin is bad, but killing a man …

I decided to clean the boat. I cleaned the floor of the engine-room. There was a lot of blood there; there was blood on the steps too. On one of the steps I found two of Bill's teeth. When I saw them I ran up onto the deck. I was sick into the sea. But I went back and I washed the steps and the floor. Then I decided to wash the deck too, the whole deck. It took me an hour. Then I cleaned the galley and the wheelhouse.

I don't know why I did all that. Perhaps it was because I felt so bad about Bill. I washed and cleaned for three hours until I was very, very tired. Then I slept.

The sun was high when I woke up the next morning. The *Eldessa* wasn't moving. I started the engine and sailed south. I didn't really know where I was.

I ate the last of the food. I knew then that I had to find land. I knew I needed a lot of luck.

And I was lucky. After three hours I saw land. It was a small island. Perhaps it was the same one as before. I wasn't sure. It didn't matter. I knew I was safe.

But I had to leave the *Eldessa*. I didn't want to answer too many questions. I got close to the island. Then I turned the *Eldessa* round and began to sail away from the island. Then I jumped into the sea.

I swam to the island and I walked to the nearest village. When I arrived there I was very tired and I needed food. The people helped me but they asked me lots of questions. I said I couldn't remember anything.

Over the next few months many people asked me hundreds of questions. I always replied that I couldn't remember anything. But that was a lie. Even now, thirty-three years later, I can remember everything. I want to forget but I can't.

Chapter Nine

The Return of the *Eldessa*

When he finished the story my father lay back in the bed. He was very tired. He closed his eyes for a few moments. But he wasn't asleep. He opened his eyes and looked at Sim again. 'Thirty-three years,' he said quietly. 'It's difficult to believe, isn't it?'

'Yes,' Sim said. Then he said, 'But what happened to you in those thirty-three years? You went to America ...'

'That's right. I wanted to go somewhere new. I wanted to start a new life. I wanted to forget all about the *Eldessa* and you and Bill. Especially Bill.

'So I went to America. I became a businessman. No more fishing. I worked hard. After three years I had my own shop. After another three years I had ten shops. I became rich.

'I got married and my wife had one son ...' – he looked at me – '... and then she died.'

'I'm sorry,' Sim said.

'Well,' my father said, 'I thought my bad luck was coming back. For a year I did nothing and then I worked harder than before. I became richer.' He smiled at me. 'At least my son will have some money.'

Sim turned to me: 'I don't know your name,' he said. 'What is it?'

'My name is Simeon,' I said.

Sim looked at me in surprise. 'Simeon ...?'

'Yes,' my father said. 'I named him Simeon because I thought you were dead.'

'You thought I was dead?'

'Yes,' my father said. 'After the last trip of the *Eldessa*, that terrible trip, I didn't want to know anything about the *Eldessa*. I wanted to forget. I didn't read the newspapers and I didn't ask questions. I thought you were all dead – Middy, Bill and you.'

'So what happened? When did you find out that I was alive?'

'Only a few weeks ago. At the end of last year I became ill. The doctor said I had only six months to live. I decided it wasn't possible to forget. I tried to find out about the *Eldessa*. I found old newspapers. I read that you did not die on that trip. I was surprised. I couldn't believe it at first. Then I thought that perhaps you were still alive. I decided to find you. I asked Simeon to help me. We decided to come back to Filder.'

'So what about you, Sim?' my father asked a few moments later. 'What have you done in these thirty-three years?'

'I've drunk a lot of wine,' Sim said. 'I've had lots of jobs, a year here, six months there, two years somewhere else ...'

'Fishing?'

'No. No fishing. I didn't want to go to sea again. No fishing, no boats.'

'I want you to start fishing again,' my father said.

Sim laughed. 'I'm too old,' he said. 'I'm sixty-three. I can't go fishing again.'

'Simeon will help you. You can teach him how to fish. He'll go with you.'

'Yes,' I said. 'I'll come with you.'

'No,' Sim said, 'it's not possible. I'm an old man. I've forgotten the sea. I haven't got a boat.'

'I'll give you a boat,' my father said. 'That isn't a problem.'

'No,' Sim said again. 'No.'

'I'll give you the best boat there is.'

'No. I can't do it.'

'I'll give you the only boat you want.'

Sim looked at my father. 'What do you mean?' he asked.

My father smiled. 'I'll give you the *Eldessa*,' he said.

'You found the *Eldessa*?' Sim said.

'Yes,' my father said. 'Well, Simeon found her.'

'Yes,' I said. 'I found the *Eldessa* two weeks ago in Branden. It was more difficult to find *you*.'

'I thought she sank years ago,' Sim said.

'No,' I said.

'But she's not in good condition,' my father said.

'No. Someone will have to repair her.' I looked at Sim.

'It's difficult to believe,' Sim said. 'She must be very old now.'

'Yes,' I said. 'Very old. But you can go to sea in her. You can go fishing again.'

'No, no!' Sim said. 'It's too late.'

'When Simeon found the *Eldessa*,' my father said, 'I decided to buy her.'

'So you're the new owner,' Sim said.

My father took a piece of paper from the table beside his bed. He gave the paper to Sim. 'No,' he said, '*you* are.'

All this happened four years ago. My father died six weeks after we found Sim. It was a difficult time for me, but Sim helped me. He helped me a lot.

Then Sim and I repaired the *Eldessa*. It took three months to do this. We worked hard. Sim became happier, younger. He stopped drinking.

We went to sea. Just Sim and I. We didn't go fishing. Fishing wasn't important. The important things were the sea, the *Eldessa* and Sim. All three together again. It was a holiday.

But Sim was right. He's too old now to be a fishing-boat captain. The *Eldessa* is too old also. So now he takes people for trips along the coast. There are comfortable cabins on the *Eldessa* and there is good food and good wine. Sim enjoys the food but he doesn't drink any of the wine.

And me? My father was wrong about me. I'm not a fisherman. I'm a businessman. I have the shops that my father gave me. I spend most of the year in America.

But once every year I come back to Filder. I rent a cabin on the *Eldessa* and Sim takes me sailing for two or three days. There is no fishing; there are no nets. Sim doesn't like fishing now. He doesn't like killing things. He only wants to sail his boat. The *Eldessa* is his again. She always has been.

The Big Catch

Exercises and Activities

Chapter 1

1 Describe in your own words what the narrator did before he met Sim. Use the pronoun 'he' instead of 'I'. You might begin:

He arrived in the port of Filder. He went to ...

The following words may help you:

then, next, afterwards.

2 Find at least two words or phrases which tell us that:

– The *Eldessa* belonged to Sim.
– Sim was successful at his job.

Chapter 2

1 Begin to write Sim's diary, giving as many dates and times as possible. (This will continue to the end of chapter 4.) Keep the entries short, but use complete sentences. Use the 24-hour clock. The diary will begin:

Monday 3rd June 1955 00.05 hours: ....

Note how many times the net was put out on Tuesday, and how many times on Wednesday before the dolphin was caught.

2 In this chapter you will find many words which refer to the weather, and different colours.
What colours do you associate with the sun, the sky, the wind and rain? And what about the sea and the waves?

Chapter 3

1 On a fishing boat, are the following things above or below the level of the sea? Look for evidence in this chapter; if no

The Big Catch

evidence is given, check any unknown words in an English dictionary.

deck; hatch(es); hold; engine; wheelhouse.

Make a drawing of a fishing-boat, showing all these features, and any others you know about.

2 What do you notice about the plural of the words 'fish' and 'herring'? Can you give the correct plural of the following nouns, without consulting a dictionary or grammar book?

sheep; cow; rabbit; trout; salmon; deer; cat; dog; sardine; goat.

3 Sim's Diary: Add your entries from Wednesday morning until Friday evening.

Chapter 4

1 Explain in your own words what a propeller is.
What has happened to the net? Why is it so difficult for the four men to solve the problem?
Write a few rules for the ideal fisherman. Each rule should begin:

He must be able to ...

2 Sim's Diary: This is the final section. Make sure you know the answers to the following questions before you continue.

 – 'In the morning': which morning?
 – 'For two days': which two days?
 – 'The next morning': which morning?
 – 'At eight o'clock in the evening': which evening?

Remember to continue using the 24-hour clock e.g. 'eight o'clock in the evening' becomes 20.00 hours.
Now your diary is complete, compare it with other students' diaries and discuss what you have included and omitted. Try to explain why these differences occur.

The Big Catch

Chapter 5

1 'The piece of wood helped me.' Can you explain how and why this was so important for Sim?

2 Two other boats – the *Rose* and the *Marsa* – help to rescue Sim. Imagine you are the captain of the *Rose* or the *Marsa*. You meet in a pub (perhaps The Old Man and the Sea). Explain to each other what you found, and what you did to help.

Chapter 6

1 This chapter is almost like a play; a few short dramatic scenes. How many 'scenes' and speakers (characters) are there? Write a short summary of each scene, and note location and characters. For example:

a The pub (The Old Man and the Sea) Sim and the narrator.
b The pub, and then the white building. ...
c ...

In groups, choose one short 'scene' each and construct a play from this chapter. Omit words such as *Sim said*. The first line will read:

SIM: That's the end of my story.

Compare your versions, and act out the dialogue, using the narrator's words to help you.

Chapter 7

1 There are now only three people on board the *Eldessa*; in Chapter 2 they were described as:

– an old man called George Millfield, known as Middy;
– a man of about thirty called Bill Shell;
– a young boy called Alan.

Do you remember who fixed the engine, and who tried to fix the radio?
Who fills each of the following roles aboard the *Eldessa*

The Big Catch

now? Refer to the text for help.

                captain; cook; jailer; navigator.

Chapter 8

1 In Chapter 4 Alan told Sim that he couldn't swim. He lied. Why? In this chapter, why does Alan jump off the *Eldessa* into the sea?

2 Where was the knife mentioned before? Do you think the knife will be important at the end of this story? Give a reason for your answer.

3 Alan kills Bill. He is a murderer. How does he do this? And how does he escape? What happens to the *Eldessa*?

Chapter 9

1 What is the narrator's name? Why do you think Alan, his father, gave him this name?

2 Who found the *Eldessa*? And who owns the *Eldessa* now?

3 How has Sim's life changed? And how old is he at the end of the story? Write Sim's diary now. How does he spend the days?

Sun. 1st July 1992 22.00 hours ...

4 Write at least one paragraph with one of the following titles:

– Life at Sea
– Wishes of a Dying Man
– Alone for thirty-three years.

The Big Catch

Glossary

Chapter 1
calm(er)   still, not rough or stormy
net   a material used for catching fish
port   a place for ships and boats to load or unload goods
pullover   a sweater
sailor(s)   a person who works on a boat or ship
sardine   a young, small fish
sink   to go down below the surface (of water)
sober   not drunk

Chapter 2
bullet(s)   capsules fired from a shotgun
dolphin   a sea animal, about 2 to 3 metres long
speed   how fast something is moving

Chapter 3
noon   twelve o'clock midday
repair   to mend, fix a broken object
splash   the sound of something hitting the water

Chapter 4
escape(d)   to get away from someone/something
fed up   cross, tired, not satisfied
miserable   unhappy, uncomfortable
rope   strong thick string

Chapter 5
coast   the land along the edge of the sea
borrow   to receive something which you will give back later
disappear(ed)   to vanish, no longer able to be seen
pub   a bar where alcohol is served
raft   a flat floating structure, usually made of wood

The Big Catch

Chapter 6
save   to rescue

Chapter 7
bacon   thin slices of salted meat from a pig
black eye   dark skin around an eye after being hit

Chapter 8
attack   to act violently against someone
choice   the chance to choose something
lie(d)   to say something untrue
step(s)   a set of surfaces built for climbing up or down
throat   the passage from the mouth into the neck

Chapter 9
condition   quality, appearance
owner   the person to whom something belongs
rent   to pay for the use of something

On a boat

below   inside a boat, under the deck
cabin   the room used for sleeping
deck   the floor of the boat
galley   the boat's kitchen
hatch   the covering for an opening in the deck
hold   the area below the deck where goods are stored
propeller   the machinery which drives the boat forward in the water
wheelhouse   the place where the captain steers the boat